Daily Affirmations

365 days of powerful affirmations for success and happiness

Table of Contents

Introduction 1

365 Daily Affirmations 3

Conclusion 99

Introduction

Thank you for choosing this book, containing 365 daily affirmations for success and happiness!

An affirmation is simply a positive statement that can help to encourage confidence, remove self-doubt, and change a person's thought patterns.

Saying an affirmation every morning is a great way to start the day! It is a chance to remind yourself that you are worthy and deserving of achieving all that you desire.

This book contains 365 of the best affirmations for success and happiness. Either go through this book from start to finish a page at a time, or simply flick to a random page every morning to choose an affirmation. Sit up straight (or stand) and repeat your day's affirmation 5-10 times. Some people like to do this while looking in the mirror, but it's totally up to you.

The important thing is that you say the affirmation as confidently as you can, with full belief in the words you are saying. Get yourself into an energetic state, puff out your chest, and repeat your affirmation with all the enthusiasm you can muster.

Saying these affirmations daily will quickly begin to produce a positive change in your life, and in no time, you'll be feeling more confident, less stressed, and more motivated than ever!

Once again, thanks for picking up this book, I hope you enjoy it!

365 Daily Affirmations

1.

Everything that is happening now is happening for my ultimate good.

2.

I have all that I need to make today a great day!

3.

I am, and always will be, enough.

4.

I am courageous. I am willing to confidently face my fears.

5.

I let go of any negative feelings about myself and acknowledge that all I can achieve whatever I set my mind to.

6.

I am capable of more than I know.

7.

I am a powerful creator. I have the power to create the life I want.

8.

I trust in my intuition and have full confidence that I will make the right decisions.

9.

I am worthy of everything I desire, and more.

10.

I am motivated by my goals and feel passionate about my work.

11.

I thrive under pressure.

12.

Every day in every way I'm getting better and better!

13.

The universe is full of unlimited opportunities for me.

14.

I can easily overcome any obstacles I face.

15.

I am surrounded by loving and positive people who want me to succeed!

16.

I am deeply grateful for everything in my life and feel truly blessed.

17.

I face new challenges with complete confidence and belief in myself.

18.

I can never fail, for everything that happens to me makes me stronger.

19.

I have the power to create positive change in my life!

20.

I feel strong, powerful, vibrant, and energetic!

21.

I am capable of far more than I know.

22.

I am deeply grateful for all the happiness and joy in my life!

23.

My self-confidence grows each and every day.

24.

I feel confident, assured, and strong.

25.

I attract success and happiness into my life.

26.

Every challenge I face is an opportunity to grow and improve.

27.

I am energetic and enthusiastic. Confidence is my natural state.

28.

I am surrounded by people who want the best for me.

29.

I can easily conquer any challenge that presents itself.

30.

I am the architect of my life; I build its foundation and select its contents.

31.

I have great ideas and make helpful contributions.

32.

I have the knowledge to make the right decisions for myself.

33.

I know and believe that today will be a great day!

34.

I am, and always will be, enough.

35.

I am the master of my fate. I am the captain of my soul.

36.

I trust my intuition to help me make the right decisions.

37.

I am living to my full potential.

38.

I have unlimited power.

39.

I have the ability to create all the success and prosperity I desire.

40.

I can easily overcome and obstacle that I face.

41.

I easily let go of negative and limiting beliefs.

42.

I celebrate every goal with gratitude and joy.

43.

I approach everything in my life with passion and enthusiasm.

44.

The world is incredibly abundant and full of opportunities for me.

45.

I can create the change I want in my life.

46.

Every day my confidence grows.

47.

I wake up every day ready for new opportunities and experiences.

48.

My success is inevitable.

49.

I am creating the life of my dreams.

50.

I can achieve anything I set my mind to.

51.

I am aligned with the energy of wealth and abundance.

52.

I excel in all that I do, and success comes easily to me.

53.

I trust that I am on the right path.

54.

I am constantly inspired by the world around me.

55.

My mind is full of brilliant ideas.

56.

I am becoming closer to my true self every day.

57.

I am focused on my goals and feel passionate about my work.

58.

I have everything I need to become successful.

59.

The universe is full of endless opportunities.

60.

Money comes to me easily and effortlessly.

61.

I attract healthy relationships into my life.

62.

I am in charge of my outcome.

63.

I can achieve anything I set my mind to.

64.

I have endless motivation.

65.

I can achieve more than anybody realizes.

66.

I am healthy, wealthy, and happy.

67.

Every day in every way I'm getting better and better.

68.

I am worthy of all things wonderful.

69.

I am growing into my fullest self.

70.

My goals are attainable, and my habits help me achieve them.

71.

My courage is more powerful than my doubt.

72.

If I put my mind to it, I can achieve it.

73.

I am willing to do what it takes to create the life of my dreams.

74.

I am a winner.

75.

I am fearless.

76.

My confidence knows no limits.

77.

I am a magnet for love.

78.

I believe fully in my talents and abilities.

79.

Prosperity flows to and through me.

80.

I am blessed beyond measure.

81.

I will never give up on my goals and dreams.

82.

I release all negativity.

83.

I have an abundance mindset.

84.

I am the master of my abundance.

85.

Today will be another successful day.

86.

I am a positive person that attracts good things.

87.

I am dependable and resourceful.

88.

I am prepared to work harder than anyone else to achieve my goals.

89.

My potential is infinite.

90.

I am worthy of all things good.

91.

I love myself fully.

92.

I am becoming who I was meant to be.

93.

I accomplish all my goals daily.

94.

I have a unique skillset that makes me valuable and important.

95.

I am worthy of all my success and accomplishments.

96.

I create the reality of my choosing.

97.

I attract the right people and circumstances into my life.

98.

I love who I am becoming.

99.

I am perfect just the way I am.

100.

I am resilient and can overcome anything.

101.

My talents are unique to me.

102.

I am open and ready to receive miracles.

103.

I am talented and intelligent.

104.

I have the power to create change.

105.

I accept myself just as I am.

106.

My possibilities are endless.

107.

I am proud of myself and all that I've accomplished.

108.

I will not compare myself to others.

109.

I deserve the best that life has to offer.

110.

Life is great and fruitful.

111.

I choose to live my life to the fullest.

112.

I love and welcome new experiences.

113.

I am a source of inspiration and motivation.

114.

I bring joy and peace to others.

115.

My challenges help me grow.

116.

I am an amazing person.

117.

I am perfect exactly as I am.

118.

I believe in myself and my abilities.

119.

I stand up for what I believe in.

120.

Today I choose to think positively.

121.

I have everything I need right now.

122.

I can make a difference.

123.

Good things are coming to me.

124.

My positive thoughts create positive feelings.

125.

Every day is a fresh start.

126.

I can be anything I want to be.

127.

I accept who I am.

128.

Today is going to be an amazing day.

129.

My business is a huge success.

130.

I am brave, bold, and beautiful.

131.

I am worthy of love.

132.

I am capable of great things.

133.

I am fine just the way I am.

134.

The past is irrelevant.

135.

I can change the world.

136.

I'm stronger than negative thoughts.

137.

I am entitled to happiness.

138.

My problems are opportunities in disguise.

139.

I inspire those around me.

140.

This is only the beginning.

141.

My inner light can't be distinguished.

142.

My strength is greater than any struggle.

143.

I am in awe of what I'm capable of.

144.

No one can make me feel inferior.

145.

I was not made to give up.

146.

I know my worth.

147.

I choose what I become.

148.

I'm brave enough to climb any mountain.

149.

I have the courage to say "no".

150.

I am deeply grateful for all that I have.

151.

I will never give up on my goals and dreams.

152.

I accomplish anything I focus on.

153.

I am dependable and resourceful.

154.

I choose prosperity over failure.

155.

Today will be another successful day.

156.

I love my body.

157.

I excel in everything I do.

158.

I live a positive life.

159.

I only attract the best situations.

160.

Success is always knocking at my door.

161.

I have unbelievable determination.

162.

I never give up.

163.

I am confident in my abilities.

164.

I am talented and intelligent.

165.

I am in control of my destiny.

166.

I am full of courage.

167.

I am a warrior.

168.

I am wonderfully and beautifully made.

169.

I acknowledge my own self-worth.

170.

I deserve to be respected.

171.

I love and respect myself deeply.

172.

I am a happy and vibrant person.

173.

I give myself permission to be happy.

174.

I am proud of who I am becoming.

175.

I am greater than any challenge.

176.

I will do big things.

177.

I am full of love.

178.

I am a magnet for positivity.

179.

Love, health, and success are attracted to me.

180.

There is always a way if I'm committed.

181.

I have unstoppable confidence.

182.

My dreams are all coming true.

183.

I am a naturally happy person.

184.

Opportunities constantly present themselves to me.

185.

I am excited about my life.

186.

I always think BIG.

187.

I am highly motivated and productive.

188.

I am manifesting everything I desire.

189.

Everything in my life happens for a reason.

190.

I act fearlessly.

191.

The universe provides me with anything I ask of it.

192.

Things have a way of working themselves out.

193.

I am blessed and highly favored.

194.

I am lucky beyond belief.

195.

I truly love who I am.

196.

I wake up each morning excited about my goals.

197.

My positive energy is contagious and inspires others.

198.

I am surrounded by abundance.

199.

My dreams are materializing before my very eyes.

200.

I am driven and ambitious.

201.

I find it easy to be optimistic.

202.

I have an attitude of gratitude.

203.

Success comes naturally to me.

204.

I only allow positive thoughts to remain in my mind.

205.

My mind is a magnet for all things good.

206.

I become what I think about.

207.

The seeds of greatness exist in my mind.

208.

I personify love, health, and happiness.

209.

My happiness is infectious.

210.

I am decisive and never hesitate to take action.

211.

It is so easy to achieve my goals.

212.

I am resilient, persistent, and dedicated.

213.

I will never give up on chasing my dreams.

214.

I continually improve in all areas of my life.

215.

My life gets better and better every day.

216.

I will achieve whatever I choose to set my mind on.

217.

I am happy, healthy, and wealthy.

218.

I am a force for positive change.

219.

I am overflowing with positive energy.

220.

My life is an exciting journey.

221.

Everywhere I go I spread joy and love.

222.

Happiness and success are automatic for me.

223.

I am destined for greatness.

224.

I can move mountains with my mind.

225.

I feel refreshed, excited, and determined to excel today.

226.

I am in charge of my life.

227.

I am confident and good at what I do.

228.

I have an unshakeable mindset.

229.

Happiness flows through me constantly.

230.

When I feel happy, I manifest more reasons to be happy.

231.

My happiness comes from within me.

232.

I see so many positives in my life.

233.

I experience joy in everything I do.

234.

I will not be discouraged by any setback I face.

235.

I am healthy, vibrant, and full of energy.

236.

I give myself permission to enjoy myself.

237.

I can create anything my heart desires.

238.

Joy is the essence of my being.

239.

I see endless positives in my life.

240.

I manifest everything my heart desires.

241.

My body is vibrant and in perfect health.

242.

I allow myself to feel good.

243.

I give myself permission to enjoy myself.

244.

The happiness I feel is felt by everyone around me.

245.

I am destined to live a happy life.

246.

I'm proud of who I'm becoming.

247.

I commit to living a happy life.

248.

I love myself and all of my flaws.

249.

I don't need validation from others.

250.

I will speak all of my dreams into existence.

251.

I am a radiant and joyous person.

252.

I love the people around me.

253.

The only person I want to be is me.

254.

Every day in every way I grow happier and happier.

255.

I am in control of my future.

256.

I am worthy of being loved.

257.

I choose to only focus on the positive.

258.

I choose how I respond to circumstances.

259.

I have full control over my emotions.

260.

I choose to feel good.

261.

I choose to feel grateful.

262.

I am proud of myself and the effort I put forth every day.

263.

I am beautifully unique.

264.

My challenges help me grow.

265.

I live life on my own terms.

266.

I am free of all worry and anxiety.

267.

I refuse to be stopped by my anxiety.

268.

I let go of any limiting thoughts and beliefs.

269.

Creativity flows naturally through me.

270.

I am willing to step out of my comfort zone to achieve my goals.

271.

My potential is unlimited.

272.

I have incredible willpower and can change my habits with ease.

273.

I am worthy of my dreams.

274.

My mind is focused and clear.

275.

My vision and purpose are clear to me.

276.

I wake up every day feeling inspired.

277.

I communicate with honesty and compassion.

278.

I am infinitely loved.

279.

I show kindness to everyone around me.

280.

My body is healthy, my heart is at peace.

281.

I am unique and irreplaceable.

282.

I am at peace with myself.

283.

I have all I need to be happy right now.

284.

I honor who I am.

285.

I am worthy of all the love and joy life has to offer.

286.

I give myself permission to thrive.

287.

Abundance flows through me.

288.

The source of my prosperity is within me.

289.

I love working towards my goals.

290.

I choose to be grateful and happy today.

291.

My heart is open and radiates joy.

292.

I allow the energy of happiness to flow through me.

293.

Day by day I am creating the life I desire.

294.

I see the good in every situation.

295.

I am beautiful, bold, and brave.

296.

Today is full of miracles.

297.

I am blessed beyond measure.

298.

Everything is happening perfectly.

299.

I accept and love myself unconditionally.

300.

I let go of any feelings of envy, jealousy, or hate.

301.

I am grateful for my happiness and positive energy.

302.

I am free to be myself.

303.

I don't allow the negative opinions of others to affect me.

304.

Everywhere I go, I attract joy.

305.

Happiness is my birthright.

306.

If I can believe it, I can achieve it.

307.

I speak my goals into existence.

308.

I welcome challenges and new opportunities.

309.

Every setback I face is an opportunity for growth.

310.

I will shock the people around me with my success.

311.

Today is my time to shine.

312.

The universe is working in my favor.

313.

I am enough.

314.

My heart is open to giving and receiving love.

315.

I am grateful for the people in my life.

316.

I am always striving to improve.

317.

I choose to be happy – no matter what.

318.

I trust my intuition.

319.

The more challenges I face, the more I grow and improve.

320.

I am bigger than my fears.

321.

I have the power to create my own reality.

322.

I am grateful for all the little things.

323.

I enjoy every moment of the day.

324.

I feel lucky to be me.

325.

For me, nothing is impossible.

326.

Love is deeply rooted in my very being.

327.

I choose to give love unconditionally.

328.

Happiness is contagious. I spread love to others and receive love from others.

329.

My life brings me deep happiness and satisfaction.

330.

Happy thoughts constantly enter my mind.

331.

I am fit, healthy, and energetic.

332.

I choose to let go of my ego.

333.

Today, I am free from suffering.

334.

Breathing in, I feel peace. Breathing out, I am peace.

335.

Nothing can dim the light that shines from within me.

336.

I know, accept, and am true to myself.

337.

I learn from my mistakes.

338.

I am superior to negative thoughts and actions.

339.

I vibrate at a high frequency.

340.

Brilliant ideas come to me effortlessly.

341.

I confidently stand up for myself and my beliefs.

342.

I am blessed to have incredible people in my life.

343.

I am admired by many people around me.

344.

My ideal future is appearing before my eyes.

345.

I have strength in my heart and clarity in my mind.

346.

My journey is only just beginning.

347.

I have an abundance mindset.

348.

I strive to be a better person each and every day.

349.

I always try my best.

350.

I respect others and their opinions.

351.

I have the knowledge necessary to succeed.

352.

Accepting help from others does not make me weak.

353.

I will not take other people's anger and negativity personally.

354.

I am confident in the presence of others.

355.

I become what I think about.

356.

I focus on what I can control and make peace with what I can't.

357.

I give thanks for all that I have, and will, achieve.

358.

I welcome abundance into my life with open arms.

359.

I am confident in my abilities.

360.

I am calm and centered.

361.

My determination is something to behold.

362.

I act bravely in the face of my fears.

363.

I let go of all that no longer serves me.

364.

Nobody can stop me from achieving my dreams.

365.

I believe in my ability to change the world.

Conclusion

Thanks again for choosing this book.

I hope you've enjoyed the affirmations contained within and will continue to use this book to bring positivity into your life.

If you enjoyed this book, please don't hesitate to share it with a friend or loved one!

Thanks again. I wish you only the best!

www.ingramcontent.com/pod-product-compliance
Lightning Source LLC
LaVergne TN
LVHW011730060526
838200LV00051B/3114